P9-DTR-518

ENCYCLICAL LETTER

DEUS CARITAS EST

OF THE SUPREME PONTIFF

BENEDICT XVI

TO THE BISHOPS
PRIESTS AND DEACONS
MEN AND WOMEN RELIGIOUS
AND ALL THE LAY FAITHFUL

ON CHRISTIAN LOVE

LIBRERIA EDITRICE VATICANA
VATICAN CITY

I Ristampa febbraio 2006

© Copyright 2006 – Libreria Editrice Vaticana – 00120 Città del Vaticano
Tel. 06.698.85003 – Fax 06.698.84716

ISBN 88-209-7788-5

www.libreriaeditricevaticana.com

INTRODUCTION

1. "GOD IS LOVE, and he who abides in love abides in God, and God abides in him" (*1 Jn* 4:16). These words from the *First Letter of John* express with remarkable clarity the heart of the Christian faith: the Christian image of God and the resulting image of mankind and its destiny. In the same verse, Saint John also offers a kind of summary of the Christian life: "We have come to know and to believe in the love God has for us."

We have come to believe in God's love: in these words the Christian can express the fundamental decision of his life. Being Christian is not the result of an ethical choice or a lofty idea, but the encounter with an event, a person, which gives life a new horizon and a decisive direction. Saint John's Gospel describes that event in these words: "God so loved the world that he gave his only Son, that whoever believes in him should ... have eternal life" (3:16). In acknowledging the centrality of love, Christian faith has retained the core of Israel's faith, while at the same time giving it new depth and breadth. The pious Jew prayed daily the words of the *Book of Deuteronomy* which expressed the heart of his existence: "Hear, O Israel: the Lord our God is one Lord, and you shall love the Lord your God with all your heart, and with all your soul and with all your might" (6:4-5). Jesus united into a single precept this commandment of love for God and the commandment of love for neighbour found in the *Book of Leviticus*: "You shall love your neighbour as yourself" (19:18; cf. *Mk* 12:29-31). Since God has first loved us (cf. *1 Jn* 4:10), love is now no longer a mere "command"; it is the response to the gift of love with which God draws near to us.

In a world where the name of God is sometimes associated with vengeance or even a duty of hatred and violence, this message is both timely and significant. For this reason, I wish in my first Encyclical to speak of the love which God lavishes upon us and which we in turn must share with others. That, in essence, is what the two main parts of this Letter are about, and they are profoundly interconnected. The first part is more speculative, since I wanted here — at the beginning of my Pontificate — to clarify some essential facts concerning the love which God mysteriously and gratuitously offers to man, together with the intrinsic link between that Love and the reality of human love. The second part is more concrete, since it treats the ecclesial exercise of the commandment of love of neighbour. The argument has vast implications, but a lengthy treatment would go beyond the scope of the present Encyclical. I wish to emphasize some basic elements, so as to call forth in the world renewed energy and commitment in the human response to God's love.

PART I

THE UNITY OF LOVE
IN CREATION
AND IN SALVATION HISTORY

A problem of language

2. God's love for us is fundamental for our lives, and it raises important questions about who God is and who we are. In considering this, we immediately find ourselves hampered by a problem of language. Today, the term "love" has become one of the most frequently used and misused of words, a word to which we attach quite different meanings. Even though this Encyclical will deal primarily with the understanding and practice of love in sacred Scripture and in the Church's Tradition, we cannot simply prescind from the meaning of the word in the different cultures and in present-day usage.

Let us first of all bring to mind the vast semantic range of the word "love": we speak of love of country, love of one's profession, love between friends, love of work, love between parents and children, love between family members, love of neighbour and love of God. Amid this multiplicity of meanings, however, one in particular stands out: love between man and woman, where body and soul are inseparably joined and human beings glimpse an apparently irresistible promise of happiness. This would seem to be the very epitome of love; all other kinds of love immediately seem to fade in comparison. So we need to ask: are all these forms of love basically one, so that love, in its many and varied manifestations, is ultimately a single reality, or are we merely using the same word to designate totally different realities?

"Eros" and "Agape" – difference and unity

3. That love between man and woman which is neither planned nor willed, but somehow imposes itself upon human beings, was called *eros* by the ancient Greeks. Let us note straight away that the Greek Old Testament uses the word *eros* only twice, while the New Testament does not use it at all: of the three Greek words for love, *eros, philia* (the love of friendship) and *agape*, New Testament writers prefer the last, which occurs rather infrequently in Greek usage. As for the term *philia*, the love of friendship, it is used with added depth of meaning in Saint John's Gospel in order to express the relationship between Jesus and his disciples. The tendency to avoid the word *eros*, together with the new vision of love expressed through the word *agape*, clearly point to something new and distinct about the Christian understanding of love. In the critique of Christianity which began with the Enlightenment and grew progressively more radical, this new element was seen as something thoroughly negative. According to Friedrich Nietzsche, Christianity had poisoned *eros*, which for its part, while not completely succumbing, gradually degenerated into vice.[1] Here the German philosopher was expressing a widely-held perception: doesn't the Church, with all her commandments and prohibitions, turn to bitterness the most precious thing in life? Doesn't she blow the whistle just when the joy which is the Creator's gift offers us a happiness which is itself a certain foretaste of the Divine?

4. But is this the case? Did Christianity really destroy *eros*? Let us take a look at the pre-

---

[1] Cf. *Jenseits von Gut und Böse*, IV, 168.

Christian world. The Greeks — not unlike other cultures — considered *eros* principally as a kind of intoxication, the overpowering of reason by a "divine madness" which tears man away from his finite existence and enables him, in the very process of being overwhelmed by divine power, to experience supreme happiness. All other powers in heaven and on earth thus appear secondary: *"Omnia vincit amor"* says Virgil in the *Bucolics* — love conquers all — and he adds: *"et nos cedamus amori"* — let us, too, yield to love.[2] In the religions, this attitude found expression in fertility cults, part of which was the "sacred" prostitution which flourished in many temples. *Eros* was thus celebrated as divine power, as fellowship with the Divine.

The Old Testament firmly opposed this form of religion, which represents a powerful temptation against monotheistic faith, combating it as a perversion of religiosity. But it in no way rejected *eros* as such; rather, it declared war on a warped and destructive form of it, because this counterfeit divinization of *eros* actually strips it of its

[2] X, 69.

dignity and dehumanizes it. Indeed, the prostitutes in the temple, who had to bestow this divine intoxication, were not treated as human beings and persons, but simply used as a means of arousing "divine madness": far from being goddesses, they were human persons being exploited. An intoxicated and undisciplined *eros*, then, is not an ascent in "ecstasy" towards the Divine, but a fall, a degradation of man. Evidently, *eros* needs to be disciplined and purified if it is to provide not just fleeting pleasure, but a certain foretaste of the pinnacle of our existence, of that beatitude for which our whole being yearns.

5. Two things emerge clearly from this rapid overview of the concept of *eros* past and present. First, there is a certain relationship between love and the Divine: love promises infinity, eternity — a reality far greater and totally other than our everyday existence. Yet we have also seen that the way to attain this goal is not simply by submitting to instinct. Purification and growth in maturity are called for; and these also pass through the path of renunciation. Far from rejecting or "poisoning" *eros*, they heal it and restore its true grandeur.

This is due first and foremost to the fact that man is a being made up of body and soul. Man is truly himself when his body and soul are intimately united; the challenge of *eros* can be said to be truly overcome when this unification is achieved. Should he aspire to be pure spirit and to reject the flesh as pertaining to his animal nature alone, then spirit and body would both lose their dignity. On the other hand, should he deny the spirit and consider matter, the body, as the only reality, he would likewise lose his greatness. The epicure Gassendi used to offer Descartes the humorous greeting: "O Soul!" And Descartes would reply: "O Flesh!" [3] Yet it is neither the spirit alone nor the body alone that loves: it is man, the person, a unified creature composed of body and soul, who loves. Only when both dimensions are truly united, does man attain his full stature. Only thus is love — *eros* — able to mature and attain its authentic grandeur.

[3] Cf. R. DESCARTES, *Œuvres*, ed. V. Cousin, vol. 12, Paris 1824, pp. 95 ff.

Nowadays Christianity of the past is often criticized as having been opposed to the body; and it is quite true that tendencies of this sort have always existed. Yet the contemporary way of exalting the body is deceptive. *Eros*, reduced to pure "sex," has become a commodity, a mere "thing" to be bought and sold, or rather, man himself becomes a commodity. This is hardly man's great "yes" to the body. On the contrary, he now considers his body and his sexuality as the purely material part of himself, to be used and exploited at will. Nor does he see it as an arena for the exercise of his freedom, but as a mere object that he attempts, as he pleases, to make both enjoyable and harmless. Here we are actually dealing with a debasement of the human body: no longer is it integrated into our overall existential freedom; no longer is it a vital expression of our whole being, but it is more or less relegated to the purely biological sphere. The apparent exaltation of the body can quickly turn into a hatred of bodiliness. Christian faith, on the other hand, has always considered man a unity in duality, a reality in which spirit and matter compenetrate, and in which each is brought to a new nobility. True, *eros* tends to rise "in ecstasy" towards the Divine, to lead us beyond ourselves; yet for this very reason it calls for a path of ascent, renunciation, purification and healing.

6. Concretely, what does this path of ascent and purification entail? How might love be experienced so that it can fully realize its human and divine promise? Here we can find a first, important indication in the *Song of Songs*, an Old Testament book well known to the mystics. According to the interpretation generally held today, the poems contained in this book were originally love-songs, perhaps intended for a Jewish wedding feast and meant to exalt conjugal love. In this context it is highly instructive to note that in the course of the book two different Hebrew words are used to indicate "love." First there is the word *dodim*, a plural form suggesting a love that is still insecure, indeterminate and searching. This comes to be replaced by the word *ahabà*, which the Greek version of the Old Testament translates with the similar-sounding *agape*, which, as we have seen, becomes the typical expression for the biblical notion of love. By contrast with an indeterminate, "searching" love, this word expresses the experience of a love which involves a real discovery of the other, moving beyond the selfish character that prevailed earlier. Love now becomes concern and care for the other. No longer is it self-seeking, a sinking in the intoxication of happiness; instead it seeks the good of the beloved: it becomes renunciation and it is ready, and even willing, for sacrifice.

It is part of love's growth towards higher levels and inward purification that it now seeks to become definitive, and it does so in a twofold sense: both in the sense of exclusivity (this particular person alone) and in the sense of being "for ever." Love embraces the whole of existence in each of its dimensions, including the dimension of time. It could hardly be otherwise, since its promise looks towards its definitive goal: love looks to the eternal. Love is indeed "ecstasy", not in the sense of a moment of intoxication, but rather as a journey, an ongoing exodus out of the closed inward-looking self towards its liberation through self-giving, and thus towards authentic self-discovery and indeed the discovery of God: "Whoever seeks to gain his life will lose it, but whoever loses his life will preserve it" (*Lk* 17:33), as Jesus says throughout the Gospels (cf. *Mt* 10:39; 16:25; *Mk* 8:35; *Lk* 9:24; *Jn* 12:25). In these words, Jesus portrays his own path, which leads through the Cross to the Resurrection: the path of the grain of wheat that falls to the ground and dies, and in this way bears much fruit. Starting from the depths of his own sacrifice and of the love that reaches fulfilment therein, he also portrays in these words the essence of love and indeed of human life itself.

7. By their own inner logic, these initial, somewhat philosophical reflections on the essence of love have now brought us to the threshold of biblical faith. We began by asking whether the different, or even opposed, meanings of the word "love" point to some profound underlying unity, or whether on the contrary they must remain unconnected, one alongside the other. More significantly, though, we questioned whether the message of love proclaimed to us by the Bible and the Church's Tradition has some points of contact with the common human experience of love, or whether it is opposed to that experience. This in turn led us to consider two fundamental words: *eros*, as a term to indicate "worldly" love and *agape*, referring to love grounded in and shaped by faith. The two notions are often contrasted as "ascending" love and "descending" love. There are other, similar classifications, such as the distinction between possessive love and oblative love (*amor concupiscentiae – amor benevolentiae*), to which is sometimes also added love that seeks its own advantage.

In philosophical and theological debate, these distinctions have often been radicalized to the point of establishing a clear antithesis between them: descending, oblative love — *agape* — would be typically Christian, while on the other hand ascending, possessive or covetous love — *eros* — would be typical of non-Christian, and particularly Greek culture. Were this antithesis to be taken to extremes, the essence of Christianity would be detached from the vital relations fundamental to human existence, and would become a world apart, admirable perhaps, but decisively cut off from the complex fabric of human life. Yet *eros* and *agape* — ascending love and descending love — can never be completely separated. The more the two, in their different aspects, find a proper unity in the one reality of love, the more the true nature of love in general is realized. Even if *eros* is at first mainly covetous and ascending, a fascination for the great promise of happiness, in drawing near to the other, it is less and less concerned with itself, increasingly seeks the happiness of the other, is concerned more and more with the beloved, bestows itself and wants to "be there for" the other. The element of *agape* thus enters into this love, for otherwise *eros* is impoverished and even loses its own nature. On the other hand, man cannot live by oblative, descending love alone. He cannot always give, he must also receive. Anyone who wishes to give love must also receive love as a gift. Certainly, as the Lord tells us, one can become a source from which rivers of living water flow (cf. *Jn* 7:37-38). Yet to become such a source, one must constantly drink anew from the original source, which is Jesus Christ, from whose pierced heart flows the love of God (cf. *Jn* 19:34).

In the account of Jacob's ladder, the Fathers of the Church saw this inseparable connection between ascending and descending love, between *eros* which seeks God and *agape* which passes on the gift received, symbolized in various ways. In that biblical passage we read how the Patriarch Jacob saw in a dream, above the stone which was his pillow, a ladder reaching up to heaven, on which the angels of God were ascending and descending (cf. *Gen* 28:12; *Jn* 1:51). A particularly striking interpretation of this vision is presented by Pope Gregory the Great in his *Pastoral Rule*. He tells us that the good pastor must be rooted in contemplation. Only in this way will he be able to take upon himself the needs of others and make them his own: *"per pietatis viscera in se infirmitatem caeterorum transferat."* [4] Saint Gregory speaks in this context of Saint Paul, who was borne aloft to the most exalted mysteries of God, and hence, having descended once more, he was able to become all things to all men (cf. *2 Cor* 12:2-4; *1 Cor* 9:22). He also points to the example of Moses, who entered the tabernacle time and again, remaining in dialogue with God, so that when he emerged he could be at the service of his people. "Within

[4] II, 5: SCh 381, 196.

[the tent] he is borne aloft through contemplation, while without he is completely engaged in helping those who suffer: *intus in contemplationem rapitur, foris infirmantium negotiis urgetur.*" [5]

8. We have thus come to an initial, albeit still somewhat generic response to the two questions raised earlier. Fundamentally, "love" is a single reality, but with different dimensions; at different times, one or other dimension may emerge more clearly. Yet when the two dimensions are totally cut off from one another, the result is a caricature or at least an impoverished form of love. And we have also seen, synthetically, that biblical faith does not set up a parallel universe, or one opposed to that primordial human phenomenon which is love, but rather accepts the whole man; it intervenes in his search for love in order to purify it and to reveal new dimensions of it. This newness of biblical faith is shown chiefly in two elements which deserve to be highlighted: the image of God and the image of man.

[5] *Ibid.*, 198.

The newness of biblical faith

9. First, the world of the Bible presents us with a new image of God. In surrounding cultures, the image of God and of the gods ultimately remained unclear and contradictory. In the development of biblical faith, however, the content of the prayer fundamental to Israel, the *Shema*, became increasingly clear and unequivocal: "Hear, O Israel, the Lord our God is one Lord" (*Dt* 6:4). There is only one God, the Creator of heaven and earth, who is thus the God of all. Two facts are significant about this statement: all other gods are not God, and the universe in which we live has its source in God and was created by him. Certainly, the notion of creation is found elsewhere, yet only here does it become absolutely clear that it is not one god among many, but the one true God himself who is the source of all that exists; the whole world comes into existence by the power of his creative Word. Consequently, his creation is dear to him, for it was willed by him and "made" by him. The second important element now emerges: this God loves man. The divine power that Aristotle at the

23

height of Greek philosophy sought to grasp through reflection, is indeed for every being an object of desire and of love — and as the object of love this divinity moves the world[6] — but in itself it lacks nothing and does not love: it is solely the object of love. The one God in whom Israel believes, on the other hand, loves with a personal love. His love, moreover, is an elective love: among all the nations he chooses Israel and loves her — but he does so precisely with a view to healing the whole human race. God loves, and his love may certainly be called *eros*, yet it is also totally *agape*.[7]

The Prophets, particularly Hosea and Ezekiel, described God's passion for his people using boldly erotic images. God's relationship with Israel is described using the metaphors of betrothal and marriage; idolatry is thus adultery and prostitution. Here we find a specific reference — as we have seen — to the fertility cults and their abuse of *eros*, but also a description of the rela-

---

[6] Cf. *Metaphysics*, XII, 7.

[7] Cf. Ps.-Dionysius the Areopagite, who in his treatise *The Divine Names,* IV, 12-14: PG 3, 709-713 calls God both *eros* and *agape*.

tionship of fidelity between Israel and her God. The history of the love-relationship between God and Israel consists, at the deepest level, in the fact that he gives her the *Torah*, thereby opening Israel's eyes to man's true nature and showing her the path leading to true humanism. It consists in the fact that man, through a life of fidelity to the one God, comes to experience himself as loved by God, and discovers joy in truth and in righteousness — a joy in God which becomes his essential happiness: "Whom do I have in heaven but you? And there is nothing upon earth that I desire besides you ... for me it is good to be near God" (*Ps* 73 [72]:25, 28).

10. We have seen that God's *eros* for man is also totally *agape*. This is not only because it is bestowed in a completely gratuitous manner, without any previous merit, but also because it is love which forgives. Hosea above all shows us that this *agape* dimension of God's love for man goes far beyond the aspect of gratuity. Israel has committed "adultery" and has broken the covenant; God should judge and repudiate her. It is precisely at this point that God is revealed to be

God and not man: "How can I give you up, O Ephraim! How can I hand you over, O Israel! ... My heart recoils within me, my compassion grows warm and tender. I will not execute my fierce anger, I will not again destroy Ephraim; for I am God and not man, the Holy One in your midst" (*Hos* 11:8-9). God's passionate love for his people — for humanity — is at the same time a forgiving love. It is so great that it turns God against himself, his love against his justice. Here Christians can see a dim prefigurement of the mystery of the Cross: so great is God's love for man that by becoming man he follows him even into death, and so reconciles justice and love.

The philosophical dimension to be noted in this biblical vision, and its importance from the standpoint of the history of religions, lies in the fact that on the one hand we find ourselves before a strictly metaphysical image of God: God is the absolute and ultimate source of all being; but this universal principle of creation — the *Logos*, primordial reason — is at the same time a lover with all the passion of a true love. *Eros* is thus supremely ennobled, yet at the same time it is so purified as to become one with *agape*. We can thus see how the reception of the *Song of Songs* in the canon of sacred Scripture was soon explained by the idea that these love songs ultimately describe God's relation to man and man's relation to God. Thus the *Song of Songs* became, both in Christian and Jewish literature, a source of mystical knowledge and experience, an expression of the essence of biblical faith: that man can indeed enter into union with God — his primordial aspiration. But this union is no mere fusion, a sinking in the nameless ocean of the Divine; it is a unity which creates love, a unity in which both God and man remain themselves and yet become fully one. As Saint Paul says: "He who is united to the Lord becomes one spirit with him" (*1 Cor* 6:17).

11. The first novelty of biblical faith consists, as we have seen, in its image of God. The second, essentially connected to this, is found in the image of man. The biblical account of creation speaks of the solitude of Adam, the first man, and God's decision to give him a helper. Of all other creatures, not one is capable of being the helper that man needs, even though he has assigned a name to all the wild beasts and birds and thus made them fully a part of his life. So God forms woman from the rib of man. Now Adam finds the helper that he needed: "This at last is bone of my bones and flesh of my flesh" (*Gen* 2:23). Here one might detect hints of ideas that are also found, for example, in the myth mentioned by Plato, according to which man was originally spherical, because he was complete in himself and self-sufficient. But as a punishment for pride, he was split in two by Zeus, so that now he longs for his other half, striving with all his being to possess it and thus regain his integrity.[8] While the biblical narrative does not speak of punishment, the idea is certainly present that man is somehow incomplete, driven by nature to seek in another the part that can make him whole, the idea that only in communion with the opposite sex can he become "complete." The biblical account thus concludes with a prophecy about Adam: "Therefore a man leaves his father and his mother and cleaves to his wife and they become one flesh" (*Gen.* 2: 24).

---

[8] PLATO, *Symposium*, XIV-XV, 189c-192d.

Two aspects of this are important. First, *eros* is somehow rooted in man's very nature; Adam is a seeker, who "abandons his mother and father" in order to find woman; only together do the two represent complete humanity and become "one flesh." The second aspect is equally important. From the standpoint of creation, *eros* directs man towards marriage, to a bond which is unique and definitive; thus, and only thus, does it fulfil its deepest purpose. Corresponding to the image of a monotheistic God is monogamous marriage. Marriage based on exclusive and definitive love becomes the icon of the relationship between God and his people and vice versa. God's way of loving becomes the measure of human love. This close connection between *eros* and marriage in the Bible has practically no equivalent in extra-biblical literature.

Jesus Christ – the incarnate love of God

12. Though up to now we have been speaking mainly of the Old Testament, nevertheless the profound compenetration of the two Testaments as the one Scripture of the Christian faith has already become evident. The real novelty of the New Testament lies not so much in new ideas as in the figure of Christ himself, who gives flesh and blood to those concepts — an unprecedented realism. In the Old Testament, the novelty of the Bible did not consist merely in abstract notions but in God's unpredictable and in some sense unprecedented activity. This divine activity now takes on dramatic form when, in Jesus Christ, it is God himself who goes in search of the "stray sheep", a suffering and lost humanity. When Jesus speaks in his parables of the shepherd who goes after the lost sheep, of the woman who looks for the lost coin, of the father who goes to meet and embrace his prodigal son, these are no mere words: they constitute an explanation of his very being and activity. His death on the Cross is the culmination of that turning of God against himself in which he gives himself in order to raise man up and save him. This is love in its most radical form. By contemplating the pierced side of Christ (cf. 19:37), we can understand the starting-point of this Encyclical Letter: "God is love" (*1 Jn* 4:8). It is there that this truth can be contemplated.

It is from there that our definition of love must begin. In this contemplation the Christian discovers the path along which his life and love must move.

13. Jesus gave this act of oblation an enduring presence through his institution of the Eucharist at the Last Supper. He anticipated his death and resurrection by giving his disciples, in the bread and wine, his very self, his body and blood as the new manna (cf. *Jn* 6:31-33). The ancient world had dimly perceived that man's real food — what truly nourishes him as man — is ultimately the *Logos*, eternal wisdom: this same *Logos* now truly becomes food for us — as love. The Eucharist draws us into Jesus' act of self-oblation. More than just statically receiving the incarnate *Logos*, we enter into the very dynamic of his self-giving. The imagery of marriage between God and Israel is now realized in a way previously inconceivable: it had meant standing in God's presence, but now it becomes union with God through sharing in Jesus' self-gift, sharing in his body and blood. The sacramental "mysticism", grounded in God's condescension towards us, operates at a radically different level and lifts us to far greater heights than anything that any human mystical elevation could ever accomplish.

14. Here we need to consider yet another aspect: this sacramental "mysticism" is social in character, for in sacramental communion I become one with the Lord, like all the other communicants. As Saint Paul says, "Because there is one bread, we who are many are one body, for we all partake of the one bread" (*1 Cor* 10:17). Union with Christ is also union with all those to whom he gives himself. I cannot possess Christ just for myself; I can belong to him only in union with all those who have become, or who will become, his own. Communion draws me out of myself towards him, and thus also towards unity with all Christians. We become "one body," completely joined in a single existence. Love of God and love of neighbour are now truly united: God incarnate draws us all to himself. We can thus understand how *agape* also became a term for the Eucharist: there God's own *agape* comes to us bodily, in order to continue his work in us and through us. Only by keeping in mind this Christological and sacramental basis can we correctly understand Jesus' teaching on love. The transition which he makes from the Law and the Prophets to the twofold commandment of love of God and of neighbour, and his grounding the whole life of faith on this central precept, is not simply a matter of morality — something that could exist apart from and alongside faith in Christ and its sacramental re-actualization. Faith, worship and *ethos* are interwoven as a single reality which takes shape in our encounter with God's *agape*. Here the usual contraposition between worship and ethics simply falls apart. "Worship" itself, Eucharistic communion, includes the reality both of being loved and of loving others in turn. A Eucharist which does not pass over into the concrete practice of love is intrinsically fragmented. Conversely, as we shall have to consider in greater detail below, the "commandment" of love is only possible because it is more than a requirement. Love can be "commanded" because it has first been given.

15. This principle is the starting-point for understanding the great parables of Jesus. The rich man (cf. *Lk* 16:19-31) begs from his place of torment that his brothers be informed about what happens to those who simply ignore the poor man in need. Jesus takes up this cry for help as a warning to help us return to the right path. The parable of the Good Samaritan (cf. *Lk* 10:25-37) offers two particularly important clarifications. Until that time, the concept of "neighbour" was understood as referring essentially to one's countrymen and to foreigners who had settled in the land of Israel; in other words, to the closely-knit community of a single country or people. This limit is now abolished. Anyone who needs me, and whom I can help, is my neighbour. The concept of "neighbour" is now universalized, yet it remains concrete. Despite being extended to all mankind, it is not reduced to a generic, abstract and undemanding expression of love, but calls for my own practical commitment here and now. The Church has the duty to interpret ever anew this relationship between near and far with regard to the actual daily life of her members. Lastly, we should especially mention the great parable of the Last Judgement (cf. *Mt* 25:31-46), in which love becomes the criterion for the definitive decision about a human life's worth or lack thereof. Jesus identifies himself with those in need, with the hungry, the thirsty, the stranger, the naked, the sick and those in prison. "As you did it to one of the least of these my brethren, you did it to me" (*Mt* 25:40). Love of God and love of neighbour have become one: in the least of the brethren we find Jesus himself, and in Jesus we find God.

Love of God and love of neighbour

16. Having reflected on the nature of love and its meaning in biblical faith, we are left with two questions concerning our own attitude: can we love God without seeing him? And can love be commanded? Against the double commandment of love these questions raise a double objection. No one has ever seen God, so how could we love him? Moreover, love cannot be commanded; it is ultimately a feeling that is either there or not, nor can it be produced by the will. Scripture seems to reinforce the first objection when it states: "If anyone says, 'I love God,' and hates his brother, he is a liar; for he who does not love his brother whom he has seen, cannot love God whom he has not seen" (*1 Jn* 4:20). But this text hardly excludes the love of God as something impossible. On the contrary, the whole context of the passage quoted from the *First Letter of John* shows that such love is explicitly demanded. The unbreakable bond between love of God and love of neighbour is emphasized. One is so closely connected to the other that to say that we love God becomes a lie if we are closed to our neighbour or hate him altogether. Saint John's words should rather be interpreted to mean that love of neighbour is a path that leads to the encounter with God, and that closing our eyes to our neighbour also blinds us to God.

17. True, no one has ever seen God as he is. And yet God is not totally invisible to us; he does not remain completely inaccessible. God loved us first, says the *Letter of John* quoted above (cf. 4:10), and this love of God has appeared in our midst. He has become visible in as much as he "has sent his only Son into the world, so that we might live through him" (*1 Jn* 4:9). God has made himself visible: in Jesus we are able to see the Father (cf. *Jn* 14:9). Indeed, God is visible in a number of ways. In the love-story recounted by the Bible, he comes towards us, he seeks to win our hearts, all the way to the Last Supper, to the piercing of his heart on the Cross, to his appearances after the Resurrection and to the great deeds by which, through the activity of the Apostles, he guided the nascent Church along its path. Nor has the Lord been absent from subsequent Church history: he encounters us ever anew, in the men and women who reflect his presence, in his word, in the sacraments, and especially in the Eucharist. In the Church's Liturgy, in her prayer, in the living community of believers, we experience the love of God, we perceive his presence and we thus learn to recognize that presence in our daily lives. He has loved us first and he continues to do so; we too, then, can respond with love. God does not demand of us a feeling which we ourselves are incapable of producing. He loves us, he makes us see and experience his love, and since he has "loved us first," love can also blossom as a response within us.

In the gradual unfolding of this encounter, it is clearly revealed that love is not merely a sentiment. Sentiments come and go. A sentiment can be a marvellous first spark, but it is not the fullness of love. Earlier we spoke of the process of purification and maturation by which *eros* comes fully into its own, becomes love in the full meaning of the word. It is characteristic of mature love that it calls into play all man's potentialities; it engages the whole man, so to speak. Contact with the visible manifestations of God's love can awaken within us a feeling of joy born of the experience of being loved. But this encounter also engages our will and our intellect. Acknowledgment of the living God is one path towards love, and the "yes" of our will to his will unites our intellect, will and sentiments in the all-embracing act of love. But this process is always open-ended; love is never "finished" and complete; throughout life, it changes and matures, and thus remains faithful to itself. *Idem velle atque idem nolle* [9] — to want the same thing, and to reject the same thing — was recognized by antiquity as the authentic

[9] SALLUST, *De coniuratione Catilinae*, XX, 4.

content of love: the one becomes similar to the other, and this leads to a community of will and thought. The love-story between God and man consists in the very fact that this communion of will increases in a communion of thought and sentiment, and thus our will and God's will increasingly coincide: God's will is no longer for me an alien will, something imposed on me from without by the commandments, but it is now my own will, based on the realization that God is in fact more deeply present to me than I am to myself.[10] Then self-abandonment to God increases and God becomes our joy (cf. *Ps* 73 [72]:23-28).

18. Love of neighbour is thus shown to be possible in the way proclaimed by the Bible, by Jesus. It consists in the very fact that, in God and with God, I love even the person whom I do not like or even know. This can only take place on the basis of an intimate encounter with God, an encounter which has become a communion of will, even affecting my feelings. Then I learn to

[10] Cf. SAINT AUGUSTINE, *Confessions*, III, 6, 11: CCL 27, 32.

look on this other person not simply with my eyes and my feelings, but from the perspective of Jesus Christ. His friend is my friend. Going beyond exterior appearances, I perceive in others an interior desire for a sign of love, of concern. This I can offer them not only through the organizations intended for such purposes, accepting it perhaps as a political necessity. Seeing with the eyes of Christ, I can give to others much more than their outward necessities; I can give them the look of love which they crave. Here we see the necessary interplay between love of God and love of neighbour which the *First Letter of John* speaks of with such insistence. If I have no contact whatsoever with God in my life, then I cannot see in the other anything more than the other, and I am incapable of seeing in him the image of God. But if in my life I fail completely to heed others, solely out of a desire to be "devout" and to perform my "religious duties", then my relationship with God will also grow arid. It becomes merely "proper," but loveless. Only my readiness to encounter my neighbour and to show him love makes me sensitive to God as well. Only if I serve my neighbour can my eyes be opened to what God does for me and how much he loves me. The saints — consider the example of Blessed Teresa of Calcutta — constantly renewed their capacity for love of neighbour from their encounter with the Eucharistic Lord, and conversely this encounter acquired its realism and depth in their service to others. Love of God and love of neighbour are thus inseparable, they form a single commandment. But both live from the love of God who has loved us first. No longer is it a question, then, of a "commandment" imposed from without and calling for the impossible, but rather of a freely-bestowed experience of love from within, a love which by its very nature must then be shared with others. Love grows through love. Love is "divine" because it comes from God and unites us to God; through this unifying process it makes us a "we" which transcends our divisions and makes us one, until in the end God is "all in all" (*1 Cor* 15:28).

PART II

CARITAS – THE PRACTICE OF LOVE
BY THE CHURCH
AS A "COMMUNITY OF LOVE"

The Church's charitable activity as a manifestation of Trinitarian love

19. "If you see charity, you see the Trinity", wrote Saint Augustine.[11] In the foregoing reflections, we have been able to focus our attention on the Pierced one (cf. *Jn* 19:37, *Zech* 12:10), recognizing the plan of the Father who, moved by love (cf. *Jn* 3:16), sent his only-begotten Son into the world to redeem man. By dying on the Cross — as Saint John tells us — Jesus "gave up his Spirit" (*Jn* 19:30), anticipating the gift of the Holy Spirit that he would make after his Resurrection (cf. *Jn* 20:22). This was to fulfil the promise of "rivers of living water" that would flow out of the hearts of believers, through the outpouring of the Spirit (cf. *Jn* 7:38-39). The Spirit, in fact, is that interior power which harmonizes their hearts with Christ's heart and moves them to love their brethren as Christ loved them, when

[11] *De Trinitate*, VIII, 8, 12: CCL 50, 287.

he bent down to wash the feet of the disciples (cf. *Jn* 13:1-13) and above all when he gave his life for us (cf. *Jn* 13:1, 15:13).

The Spirit is also the energy which transforms the heart of the ecclesial community, so that it becomes a witness before the world to the love of the Father, who wishes to make humanity a single family in his Son. The entire activity of the Church is an expression of a love that seeks the integral good of man: it seeks his evangelization through Word and Sacrament, an undertaking that is often heroic in the way it is acted out in history; and it seeks to promote man in the various arenas of life and human activity. Love is therefore the service that the Church carries out in order to attend constantly to man's sufferings and his needs, including material needs. And this is the aspect, this *service of charity*, on which I want to focus in the second part of the Encyclical.

Charity as a responsibility of the Church

20. Love of neighbour, grounded in the love of God, is first and foremost a responsibility for each individual member of the faithful, but it is also a responsibility for the entire ecclesial community at every level: from the local community to the particular Church and to the Church universal in its entirety. As a community, the Church must practise love. Love thus needs to be organized if it is to be an ordered service to the community. The awareness of this responsibility has had a constitutive relevance in the Church from the beginning: "All who believed were together and had all things in common; and they sold their possessions and goods and distributed them to all, as any had need" (*Acts* 2:44-5). In these words, Saint Luke provides a kind of definition of the Church, whose constitutive elements include fidelity to the "teaching of the Apostles," "communion" (*koinonia*), "the breaking of the bread" and "prayer" (cf. *Acts* 2:42). The element of "communion" (*koinonia*) is not initially defined, but appears concretely in the verses quoted above: it consists in the fact that believers hold all things in common and that among them, there is no longer any distinction between rich and poor (cf. also *Acts* 4:32-37). As the Church grew, this radical form of material communion could not in fact be preserved. But its essential

47

core remained: within the community of believers there can never be room for a poverty that denies anyone what is needed for a dignified life.

21. A decisive step in the difficult search for ways of putting this fundamental ecclesial principle into practice is illustrated in the choice of the seven, which marked the origin of the diaconal office (cf. *Acts* 6:5-6). In the early Church, in fact, with regard to the daily distribution to widows, a disparity had arisen between Hebrew speakers and Greek speakers. The Apostles, who had been entrusted primarily with "prayer" (the Eucharist and the liturgy) and the "ministry of the word," felt over-burdened by "serving tables," so they decided to reserve to themselves the principal duty and to designate for the other task, also necessary in the Church, a group of seven persons. Nor was this group to carry out a purely mechanical work of distribution: they were to be men "full of the Spirit and of wisdom" (cf. *Acts* 6:1-6). In other words, the social service which they were meant to provide was absolutely concrete, yet at the same time it was also a spiritual service; theirs was a truly spiritual office which carried out an essential responsibility of the Church, namely a well-ordered love of neighbour. With the formation of this group of seven, "*diaconia*" — the ministry of charity exercised in a communitarian, orderly way — became part of the fundamental structure of the Church.

22. As the years went by and the Church spread further afield, the exercise of charity became established as one of her essential activities, along with the administration of the sacraments and the proclamation of the word: love for widows and orphans, prisoners, and the sick and needy of every kind, is as essential to her as the ministry of the sacraments and preaching of the Gospel. The Church cannot neglect the service of charity any more than she can neglect the Sacraments and the Word. A few references will suffice to demonstrate this. Justin Martyr († *c.* 155) in speaking of the Christians' celebration of Sunday, also mentions their charitable activity, linked with the Eucharist as such. Those who are able make offerings in accordance with their means, each as he or she wishes; the Bishop in turn makes use of these to support orphans, widows, the sick and those who for other reasons find themselves in need, such as prisoners and foreigners.[12] The great Christian writer Tertullian († after 220) relates how the pagans were struck by the Christians' concern for the needy of every sort.[13] And when Ignatius of Antioch († *c.* 117) described the Church of Rome as "presiding in charity (*agape*)",[14] we may assume that with this definition he also intended in some sense to express her concrete charitable activity.

23. Here it might be helpful to allude to the earliest legal structures associated with the service of charity in the Church. Towards the middle of the fourth century we see the development in Egypt of the "*diaconia*": the institution within each monastery responsible for all works of relief, that is to say, for the service of charity. By the sixth century this institution had evolved into a corporation with full juridical standing, which the civil authorities themselves entrusted with part

---

[12] Cf. *I Apologia,* 67: PG 6, 429.
[13] Cf. *Apologeticum,* 39, 7: PL 1, 468.
[14] *Ep. ad Rom., Inscr:* PG 5, 801.

of the grain for public distribution. In Egypt not only each monastery, but each individual Diocese eventually had its own *diaconia*; this institution then developed in both East and West. Pope Gregory the Great († 604) mentions the *diaconia* of Naples, while in Rome the *diaconiae* are documented from the seventh and eighth centuries. But charitable activity on behalf of the poor and suffering was naturally an essential part of the Church of Rome from the very beginning, based on the principles of Christian life given in the *Acts of the Apostles*. It found a vivid expression in the case of the deacon Lawrence († 258). The dramatic description of Lawrence's martyrdom was known to Saint Ambrose († 397) and it provides a fundamentally authentic picture of the saint. As the one responsible for the care of the poor in Rome, Lawrence had been given a period of time, after the capture of the Pope and of Lawrence's fellow deacons, to collect the treasures of the Church and hand them over to the civil authorities. He distributed to the poor whatever funds were available and then presented to the authorities the poor themselves as the real treasure of the Church.[15] Whatever historical reliability one attributes to these details, Lawrence has always remained present in the Church's memory as a great exponent of ecclesial charity.

24. A mention of the emperor Julian the Apostate († 363) can also show how essential the early Church considered the organized practice of charity. As a child of six years, Julian witnessed the assassination of his father, brother and other family members by the guards of the imperial palace; rightly or wrongly, he blamed this brutal act on the Emperor Constantius, who passed himself off as an outstanding Christian. The Christian faith was thus definitively discredited in his eyes. Upon becoming emperor, Julian decided to restore paganism, the ancient Roman religion, while reforming it in the hope of making it the driving force behind the empire. In this project he was amply inspired by Christianity. He established a hierarchy of metropolitans and priests who were to foster love of God and

---

[15] Cf. Saint Ambrose, *De officiis ministrorum*, II, 28, 140: PL 16, 141.

neighbour. In one of his letters,[16] he wrote that the sole aspect of Christianity which had impressed him was the Church's charitable activity. He thus considered it essential for his new pagan religion that, alongside the system of the Church's charity, an equivalent activity of its own be established. According to him, this was the reason for the popularity of the "Galileans." They needed now to be imitated and outdone. In this way, then, the Emperor confirmed that charity was a decisive feature of the Christian community, the Church.

25. Thus far, two essential facts have emerged from our reflections:

a) The Church's deepest nature is expressed in her three-fold responsibility: of proclaiming the word of God (*kerygma-martyria*), celebrating the sacraments (*leitourgia*), and exercising the ministry of charity (*diakonia*). These duties presuppose each other and are inseparable. For the Church, charity is not a kind of welfare activity

---

[16] Cf. *Ep.* 83: J. Bidez, *L'Empereur Julien. Œuvres complètes*, Paris 1960^2, v. I, 2^a, p. 145.

which could equally well be left to others, but is a part of her nature, an indispensable expression of her very being.[17]

b) The Church is God's family in the world. In this family no one ought to go without the necessities of life. Yet at the same time *caritas-agape* extends beyond the frontiers of the Church. The parable of the Good Samaritan remains as a standard which imposes universal love towards the needy whom we encounter "by chance" (cf. *Lk* 10:31), whoever they may be. Without in any way detracting from this commandment of universal love, the Church also has a specific responsibility: within the ecclesial family no member should suffer through being in need. The teaching of the *Letter to the Galatians* is emphatic: "So then, as we have opportunity, let us do good to all, and especially to those who are of the household of faith" (6:10).

---

[17] Cf. CONGREGATION FOR BISHOPS, Directory for the Pastoral Ministry of Bishops *Apostolorum Successores* (22 February 2004), 194, Vatican City, 2004, p. 213.

Justice and Charity

26. Since the nineteenth century, an objection has been raised to the Church's charitable activity, subsequently developed with particular insistence by Marxism: the poor, it is claimed, do not need charity but justice. Works of charity — almsgiving — are in effect a way for the rich to shirk their obligation to work for justice and a means of soothing their consciences, while preserving their own status and robbing the poor of their rights. Instead of contributing through individual works of charity to maintaining the *status quo*, we need to build a just social order in which all receive their share of the world's goods and no longer have to depend on charity. There is admittedly some truth to this argument, but also much that is mistaken. It is true that the pursuit of justice must be a fundamental norm of the State and that the aim of a just social order is to guarantee to each person, according to the principle of subsidiarity, his share of the community's goods. This has always been emphasized by Christian teaching on the State and by the Church's social doctrine. Historically, the issue of the just ordering of the collectivity had taken a new dimension with the industrialization of society in the nineteenth century. The rise of modern industry caused the old social structures to collapse, while the growth of a class of salaried workers provoked radical changes in the fabric of society. The relationship between capital and labour now became the decisive issue — an issue which in that form was previously unknown. Capital and the means of production were now the new source of power which, concentrated in the hands of a few, led to the suppression of the rights of the working classes, against which they had to rebel.

27. It must be admitted that the Church's leadership was slow to realize that the issue of the just structuring of society needed to be approached in a new way. There were some pioneers, such as Bishop Ketteler of Mainz († 1877), and concrete needs were met by a growing number of groups, associations, leagues, federations and, in particular, by the new religious orders founded in the nineteenth century to combat poverty, disease and the need for better education. In 1891, the papal magisterium intervened with the Encyclical *Rerum Novarum* of Leo XIII. This was followed in 1931 by Pius XI's Encyclical *Quadragesimo Anno*. In 1961 Blessed John XXIII published the Encyclical *Mater et Magistra*, while Paul VI, in the Encyclical *Populorum Progressio* (1967) and in the Apostolic Letter *Octogesima Adveniens* (1971), insistently addressed the social problem, which had meanwhile become especially acute in Latin America. My great predecessor John Paul II left us a trilogy of social Encyclicals: *Laborem Exercens* (1981), *Sollicitudo Rei Socialis* (1987) and finally *Centesimus Annus* (1991). Faced with new situations and issues, Catholic social teaching thus gradually developed, and has now found a comprehensive presentation in the *Compendium of the Social Doctrine of the Church* published in 2004 by the Pontifical Council *Iustitia et Pax*. Marxism had seen world revolution and its preliminaries as the panacea for the social problem: revolution and the subsequent collectivization of the means of production, so it was claimed, would immediately change things for the better. This illusion has vanished. In today's complex situation, not least because of the growth of a globalized economy, the Church's social doctrine has become a set of fundamental guidelines offering approaches that are valid even beyond the confines of the Church: in the face of ongoing development these guidelines need to be addressed in the context of dialogue with all those seriously concerned for humanity and for the world in which we live.

28. In order to define more accurately the relationship between the necessary commitment to justice and the ministry of charity, two fundamental situations need to be considered:

a) The just ordering of society and the State is a central responsibility of politics. As Augustine once said, a State which is not governed according to justice would be just a bunch of thieves: *"Remota itaque iustitia quid sunt regna nisi magna latrocinia?"*.[18] Fundamental to Christianity is the distinction between what belongs to Caesar and what belongs to God (cf. *Mt* 22:21), in other words, the distinction between Church and State, or, as the Second Vatican Council puts it, the

---

[18] *De Civitate Dei*, IV, 4: CCL 47, 102.

autonomy of the temporal sphere.[19] The State may not impose religion, yet it must guarantee religious freedom and harmony between the followers of different religions. For her part, the Church, as the social expression of Christian faith, has a proper independence and is structured on the basis of her faith as a community which the State must recognize. The two spheres are distinct, yet always interrelated.

Justice is both the aim and the intrinsic criterion of all politics. Politics is more than a mere mechanism for defining the rules of public life: its origin and its goal are found in justice, which by its very nature has to do with ethics. The State must inevitably face the question of how justice can be achieved here and now. But this presupposes an even more radical question: what is justice? The problem is one of practical reason; but if reason is to be exercised properly, it must undergo constant purification, since it can never be completely free of the danger of a certain ethical

[19] Cf. Pastoral Constitution on the Church in the Modern World *Gaudium et Spes*, 36.

blindness caused by the dazzling effect of power and special interests.

Here politics and faith meet. Faith by its specific nature is an encounter with the living God — an encounter opening up new horizons extending beyond the sphere of reason. But it is also a purifying force for reason itself. From God's standpoint, faith liberates reason from its blind spots and therefore helps it to be ever more fully itself. Faith enables reason to do its work more effectively and to see its proper object more clearly. This is where Catholic social doctrine has its place: it has no intention of giving the Church power over the State. Even less is it an attempt to impose on those who do not share the faith ways of thinking and modes of conduct proper to faith. Its aim is simply to help purify reason and to contribute, here and now, to the acknowledgment and attainment of what is just.

The Church's social teaching argues on the basis of reason and natural law, namely, on the basis of what is in accord with the nature of every human being. It recognizes that it is not the Church's responsibility to make this teaching prevail in political life. Rather, the Church wishes to help form consciences in political life and to sti mulate greater insight into the authentic require- ments of justice as well as greater readiness to act accordingly, even when this might involve con- flict with situations of personal interest. Building a just social and civil order, wherein each person receives what is his or her due, is an essential task which every generation must take up anew. As a political task, this cannot be the Church's im- mediate responsibility. Yet, since it is also a most important human responsibility, the Church is duty-bound to offer, through the purification of reason and through ethical formation, her own specific contribution towards understanding the requirements of justice and achieving them polit- ically.

The Church cannot and must not take upon herself the political battle to bring about the most just society possible. She cannot and must not replace the State. Yet at the same time she cannot and must not remain on the sidelines in the fight for justice. She has to play her part through rational argument and she has to reawaken the spiritual energy without which justice, which always demands sacrifice, cannot prevail and prosper. A just society must be the achievement of politics, not of the Church. Yet the promotion of justice through efforts to bring about openness of mind and will to the demands of the common good is something which concerns the Church deeply.

b) Love — *caritas* — will always prove necessary, even in the most just society. There is no ordering of the State so just that it can eliminate the need for a service of love. Whoever wants to eliminate love is preparing to eliminate man as such. There will always be suffering which cries out for consolation and help. There will always be loneliness. There will always be situations of material need where help in the form of concrete love of neighbour is indispensable.[20] The State which would provide everything, absorbing everything into itself, would ultimately become a mere bureaucracy incapable of guaranteeing the very thing which the suffering person — every person — needs: namely, loving personal concern. We do not need a State which regulates

---

[20] Cf. CONGREGATION FOR BISHOPS, Directory for the Pastoral Ministry of Bishops *Apostolorum Successores* (22 February 2004), 197, Vatican City, 2004, p. 217.

and controls everything, but a State which, in accordance with the principle of subsidiarity, generously acknowledges and supports initiatives arising from the different social forces and combines spontaneity with closeness to those in need. The Church is one of those living forces: she is alive with the love enkindled by the Spirit of Christ. This love does not simply offer people material help, but refreshment and care for their souls, something which often is even more necessary than material support. In the end, the claim that just social structures would make works of charity superfluous masks a materialist conception of man: the mistaken notion that man can live "by bread alone" (*Mt* 4:4; cf. *Dt* 8:3) — a conviction that demeans man and ultimately disregards all that is specifically human.

29. We can now determine more precisely, in the life of the Church, the relationship between commitment to the just ordering of the State and society on the one hand, and organized charitable activity on the other. We have seen that the formation of just structures is not directly the duty of the Church, but belongs to the world of politics, the sphere of the autonomous use of reason. The Church has an indirect duty here, in that she is called to contribute to the purification of reason and to the reawakening of those moral forces without which just structures are neither established nor prove effective in the long run.

The direct duty to work for a just ordering of society, on the other hand, is proper to the lay faithful. As citizens of the State, they are called to take part in public life in a personal capacity. So they cannot relinquish their participation "in the many different economic, social, legislative, administrative and cultural areas, which are intended to promote organically and institutionally the *common good*."[21] The mission of the lay faithful is therefore to configure social life correctly, respecting its legitimate autonomy and cooperating with other citizens according to their respective competences and fulfilling their own responsibility.[22] Even if the specific expressions

---

[21] JOHN PAUL II, Post-Synodal Apostolic Exhortation *Christifideles Laici* (30 December 1988), 42: AAS 81 (1989), 472.

[22] Cf. CONGREGATION FOR THE DOCTRINE OF THE FAITH, *Doctrinal Note on Some Questions Regarding the Participation of Catholics in Political Life* (24 November 2002), 1: *L'Osservatore Romano*, English edition, 22 January 2003, p. 5.

of ecclesial charity can never be confused with the activity of the State, it still remains true that charity must animate the entire lives of the lay faithful and therefore also their political activity, lived as "social charity." [23]

The Church's charitable organizations, on the other hand, constitute an *opus proprium*, a task agreeable to her, in which she does not cooperate collaterally, but acts as a subject with direct responsibility, doing what corresponds to her nature. The Church can never be exempted from practising charity as an organized activity of believers, and on the other hand, there will never be a situation where the charity of each individual Christian is unnecessary, because in addition to justice man needs, and will always need, love.

The multiple structures of charitable service in the social context of the present day

30. Before attempting to define the specific profile of the Church's activities in the service of man, I now wish to consider the overall situation of the struggle for justice and love in the world of today.

[23] *Catechism of the Catholic Church*, 1939.

a) Today the means of mass communication have made our planet smaller, rapidly narrowing the distance between different peoples and cultures. This "togetherness" at times gives rise to misunderstandings and tensions, yet our ability to know almost instantly about the needs of others challenges us to share their situation and their difficulties. Despite the great advances made in science and technology, each day we see how much suffering there is in the world on account of different kinds of poverty, both material and spiritual. Our times call for a new readiness to assist our neighbours in need. The Second Vatican Council had made this point very clearly: "Now that, through better means of communication, distances between peoples have been almost eliminated, charitable activity can and should embrace all people and all needs." [24]

On the other hand — and here we see one of the challenging yet also positive sides of the process of globalization — we now have at our disposal numerous means for offering humanitarian

[24] Decree on the Apostolate of the Laity *Apostolicam Actuositatem*, 8.

assistance to our brothers and sisters in need, not least modern systems of distributing food and clothing, and of providing housing and care. Concern for our neighbour transcends the confines of national communities and has increasingly broadened its horizon to the whole world. The Second Vatican Council rightly observed that "among the signs of our times, one particularly worthy of note is a growing, inescapable sense of solidarity between all peoples."[25] State agencies and humanitarian associations work to promote this, the former mainly through subsidies or tax relief, the latter by making available considerable resources. The solidarity shown by civil society thus significantly surpasses that shown by individuals.

b) This situation has led to the birth and the growth of many forms of cooperation between State and Church agencies, which have borne fruit. Church agencies, with their transparent operation and their faithfulness to the duty of witnessing to love, are able to give a Christian quality to the civil agencies too, favouring a mutual

[25] *Ibid.*, 14.

coordination that can only redound to the effectiveness of charitable service.[26] Numerous organizations for charitable or philanthropic purposes have also been established and these are committed to achieving adequate humanitarian solutions to the social and political problems of the day. Significantly, our time has also seen the growth and spread of different kinds of volunteer work, which assume responsibility for providing a variety of services.[27] I wish here to offer a special word of gratitude and appreciation to all those who take part in these activities in whatever way. For young people, this widespread involvement constitutes a school of life which offers them a formation in solidarity and in readiness to offer others not simply material aid but their very selves. The anti-culture of death, which finds expression for example in drug use, is thus countered by an unselfish love which shows itself to

[26] Cf. CONGREGATION FOR BISHOPS, Directory for the Pastoral Ministry of Bishops *Apostolorum Successores* (22 February 2004), 195, Vatican City, 2004, pp. 214-216.

[27] Cf. JOHN PAUL II, Post-Synodal Apostolic Exhortation *Christifideles Laici* (30 December 1988), 41: AAS 81 (1989), 470-472.

be a culture of life by the very willingness to "lose itself" (cf. *Lk* 17:33 *et passim*) for others.

In the Catholic Church, and also in the other Churches and Ecclesial Communities, new forms of charitable activity have arisen, while other, older ones have taken on new life and energy. In these new forms, it is often possible to establish a fruitful link between evangelization and works of charity. Here I would clearly reaffirm what my great predecessor John Paul II wrote in his Encyclical *Sollicitudo Rei Socialis* [28] when he asserted the readiness of the Catholic Church to cooperate with the charitable agencies of these Churches and Communities, since we all have the same fundamental motivation and look towards the same goal: a true humanism, which acknowledges that man is made in the image of God and wants to help him to live in a way consonant with that dignity. His Encyclical *Ut Unum Sint* emphasized that the building of a better world requires Christians to speak with a united voice in working to inculcate "respect for the rights and needs of everyone, especially the poor,

---

[28] Cf. No. 32: AAS 80 (1988), 556.

the lowly and the defenceless."[29] Here I would like to express my satisfaction that this appeal has found a wide resonance in numerous initiatives throughout the world.

The distinctiveness of the Church's charitable activity

31. The increase in diversified organizations engaged in meeting various human needs is ultimately due to the fact that the command of love of neighbour is inscribed by the Creator in man's very nature. It is also a result of the presence of Christianity in the world, since Christianity constantly revives and acts out this imperative, so often profoundly obscured in the course of time. The reform of paganism attempted by the emperor Julian the Apostate is only an initial example of this effect; here we see how the power of Christianity spread well beyond the frontiers of the Christian faith. For this reason, it is very important that the Church's charitable activity maintains all of its splendour and does not be-

[29] No. 43: AAS 87 (1995), 946.

come just another form of social assistance. So what are the essential elements of Christian and ecclesial charity?

a) Following the example given in the parable of the Good Samaritan, Christian charity is first of all the simple response to immediate needs and specific situations: feeding the hungry, clothing the naked, caring for and healing the sick, visiting those in prison, etc. The Church's charitable organizations, beginning with those of *Caritas* (at diocesan, national and international levels), ought to do everything in their power to provide the resources and above all the personnel needed for this work. Individuals who care for those in need must first be professionally competent: they should be properly trained in what to do and how to do it, and committed to continuing care. Yet, while professional competence is a primary, fundamental requirement, it is not of itself sufficient. We are dealing with human beings, and human beings always need something more than technically proper care. They need humanity. They need heartfelt concern. Those who work for the Church's charitable organizations must be distinguished by the fact that they do not merely meet the needs of the moment, but they dedicate themselves to others with heartfelt concern, enabling them to experience the richness of their humanity. Consequently, in addition to their necessary professional training, these charity workers need a "formation of the heart": they need to be led to that encounter with God in Christ which awakens their love and opens their spirits to others. As a result, love of neighbour will no longer be for them a commandment imposed, so to speak, from without, but a consequence deriving from their faith, a faith which becomes active through love (cf. *Gal* 5:6).

b) Christian charitable activity must be independent of parties and ideologies. It is not a means of changing the world ideologically, and it is not at the service of worldly stratagems, but it is a way of making present here and now the love which man always needs. The modern age, particularly from the nineteenth century on, has been dominated by various versions of a philosophy of progress whose most radical form is Marxism. Part of Marxist strategy is the theory of impoverishment: in a situation of unjust power, it is claimed, anyone who engages in charitable initiatives is actually serving that unjust system, making it appear at least to some extent tolerable. This in turn slows down a potential revolution and thus blocks the struggle for a better world. Seen in this way, charity is rejected and attacked as a means of preserving the *status quo*. What we have here, though, is really an inhuman philosophy. People of the present are sacrificed to the *moloch* of the future — a future whose effective realization is at best doubtful. One does not make the world more human by refusing to act humanely here and now. We contribute to a better world only by personally doing good now, with full commitment and wherever we have the opportunity, independently of partisan strategies and programmes. The Christian's programme — the programme of the Good Samaritan, the programme of Jesus — is "a heart which sees." This heart sees where love is needed and acts accordingly. Obviously when charitable activity is carried out by the Church as a communitarian initiative, the spontaneity of individuals must be combined with planning, foresight and cooperation with other similar institutions.

c) Charity, furthermore, cannot be used as a means of engaging in what is nowadays considered proselytism. Love is free; it is not practised as a way of achieving other ends.[30] But this does not mean that charitable activity must somehow leave God and Christ aside. For it is always concerned with the whole man. Often the deepest cause of suffering is the very absence of God. Those who practise charity in the Church's name will never seek to impose the Church's faith upon others. They realize that a pure and generous love is the best witness to the God in whom we believe and by whom we are driven to love. A Christian knows when it is time to speak of God and when it is better to say nothing and to let love alone speak. He knows that God is love (cf. *1 Jn* 4:8) and that God's presence is felt at the very time when the only thing we do is to love. He knows — to return to the questions raised earlier — that disdain for love is disdain for God and man alike; it is an attempt to do without God. Consequently, the best defence of

[30] Cf. CONGREGATION FOR BISHOPS, Directory for the Pastoral Ministry of Bishops *Apostolorum Successores* (22 February 2004), 196, Vatican City, 2004, p. 216.

God and man consists precisely in love. It is the responsibility of the Church's charitable organizations to reinforce this awareness in their members, so that by their activity — as well as their words, their silence, their example — they may be credible witnesses to Christ.

Those responsible for the Church's charitable activity

32. Finally, we must turn our attention once again to those who are responsible for carrying out the Church's charitable activity. As our preceding reflections have made clear, the true subject of the various Catholic organizations that carry out a ministry of charity is the Church herself — at all levels, from the parishes, through the particular Churches, to the universal Church. For this reason it was most opportune that my venerable predecessor Paul VI established the Pontifical Council *Cor Unum* as the agency of the Holy See responsible for orienting and coordinating the organizations and charitable activities promoted by the Catholic Church. In conformity with the episcopal structure of the Church, the

Bishops, as successors of the Apostles, are charged with primary responsibility for carrying out in the particular Churches the programme set forth in the *Acts of the Apostles* (cf. 2:42-44): today as in the past, the Church as God's family must be a place where help is given and received, and at the same time, a place where people are also prepared to serve those outside her confines who are in need of help. In the rite of episcopal ordination, prior to the act of consecration itself, the candidate must respond to several questions which express the essential elements of his office and recall the duties of his future ministry. He promises expressly to be, in the Lord's name, welcoming and merciful to the poor and to all those in need of consolation and assistance.[31] The *Code of Canon Law*, in the canons on the ministry of the Bishop, does not expressly mention charity as a specific sector of episcopal activity, but speaks in general terms of the Bishop's responsibility for coordinating the different works of the apostolate with due regard for their proper char-

---

[31] Cf. Pontificale Romanum, *De ordinatione episcopi*, 43.

acter.[32] Recently, however, the *Directory for the Pastoral Ministry of Bishops* explored more specifically the duty of charity as a responsibility incumbent upon the whole Church and upon each Bishop in his Diocese,[33] and it emphasized that the exercise of charity is an action of the Church as such, and that, like the ministry of Word and Sacrament, it too has been an essential part of her mission from the very beginning.[34]

33. With regard to the personnel who carry out the Church's charitable activity on the practical level, the essential has already been said: they must not be inspired by ideologies aimed at improving the world, but should rather be guided by the faith which works through love (cf. *Gal* 5:6). Consequently, more than anything, they must be persons moved by Christ's love, persons whose hearts Christ has conquered with his love, awakening within them a love of neighbour. The

[32] Cf. can. 394; *Code of Canons of the Eastern Churches*, can. 203.
[33] Cf. Nos. 193-198: pp. 212-219.
[34] *Ibid.*, 194: pp. 213-214.

criterion inspiring their activity should be Saint Paul's statement in the *Second Letter to the Corinthians*: "the love of Christ urges us on" (5:14). The consciousness that, in Christ, God has given himself for us, even unto death, must inspire us to live no longer for ourselves but for him, and, with him, for others. Whoever loves Christ loves the Church, and desires the Church to be increasingly the image and instrument of the love which flows from Christ. The personnel of every Catholic charitable organization want to work with the Church and therefore with the Bishop, so that the love of God can spread throughout the world. By their sharing in the Church's practice of love, they wish to be witnesses of God and of Christ, and they wish for this very reason freely to do good to all.

34. Interior openness to the Catholic dimension of the Church cannot fail to dispose charity workers to work in harmony with other organizations in serving various forms of need, but in a way that respects what is distinctive about the service which Christ requested of his disciples.

Saint Paul, in his hymn to charity (cf. *1 Cor* 13), teaches us that it is always more than activity alone: "If I give away all I have, and if I deliver my body to be burned, but do not have love, I gain nothing" (v. 3). This hymn must be the *Magna Carta* of all ecclesial service; it sums up all the reflections on love which I have offered throughout this Encyclical Letter. Practical activity will always be insufficient, unless it visibly expresses a love for man, a love nourished by an encounter with Christ. My deep personal sharing in the needs and sufferings of others becomes a sharing of my very self with them: if my gift is not to prove a source of humiliation, I must give to others not only something that is my own, but my very self; I must be personally present in my gift.

35. This proper way of serving others also leads to humility. The one who serves does not consider himself superior to the one served, however miserable his situation at the moment may be. Christ took the lowest place in the world — the Cross — and by this radical humility he redeemed us and constantly comes to our aid.

Those who are in a position to help others will realize that in doing so they themselves receive help; being able to help others is no merit or achievement of their own. This duty is a grace. The more we do for others, the more we understand and can appropriate the words of Christ: "We are useless servants" (*Lk* 17:10). We recognize that we are not acting on the basis of any superiority or greater personal efficiency, but because the Lord has graciously enabled us to do so. There are times when the burden of need and our own limitations might tempt us to become discouraged. But precisely then we are helped by the knowledge that, in the end, we are only instruments in the Lord's hands; and this knowledge frees us from the presumption of thinking that we alone are personally responsible for building a better world. In all humility we will do what we can, and in all humility we will entrust the rest to the Lord. It is God who governs the world, not we. We offer him our service only to the extent that we can, and for as long as he grants us the strength. To do all we can with what strength we have, however, is the task which keeps the good servant of Jesus Christ always at work: "The love of Christ urges us on" (*2 Cor* 5:14).

36. When we consider the immensity of others' needs, we can, on the one hand, be driven towards an ideology that would aim at doing what God's governance of the world apparently cannot: fully resolving every problem. Or we can be tempted to give in to inertia, since it would seem that in any event nothing can be accomplished. At such times, a living relationship with Christ is decisive if we are to keep on the right path, without falling into an arrogant contempt for man, something not only unconstructive but actually destructive, or surrendering to a resignation which would prevent us from being guided by love in the service of others. Prayer, as a means of drawing ever new strength from Christ, is concretely and urgently needed. People who pray are not wasting their time, even though the situation appears desperate and seems to call for action alone. Piety does not undermine the struggle against the poverty of our neighbours, however extreme. In the example of Blessed

Teresa of Calcutta we have a clear illustration of the fact that time devoted to God in prayer not only does not detract from effective and loving service to our neighbour but is in fact the inexhaustible source of that service. In her letter for Lent 1996, Blessed Teresa wrote to her lay co-workers: "We need this deep connection with God in our daily life. How can we obtain it? By prayer."

37. It is time to reaffirm the importance of prayer in the face of the activism and the growing secularism of many Christians engaged in charitable work. Clearly, the Christian who prays does not claim to be able to change God's plans or correct what he has foreseen. Rather, he seeks an encounter with the Father of Jesus Christ, asking God to be present with the consolation of the Spirit to him and his work. A personal relationship with God and an abandonment to his will can prevent man from being demeaned and save him from falling prey to the teaching of fanaticism and terrorism. An authentically religious attitude prevents man from presuming to judge

God, accusing him of allowing poverty and failing to have compassion for his creatures. When people claim to build a case against God in defence of man, on whom can they depend when human activity proves powerless?

38. Certainly Job could complain before God about the presence of incomprehensible and apparently unjustified suffering in the world. In his pain he cried out: "Oh, that I knew where I might find him, that I might come even to his seat! ... I would learn what he would answer me, and understand what he would say to me. Would he contend with me in the greatness of his power? ... Therefore I am terrified at his presence; when I consider, I am in dread of him. God has made my heart faint; the Almighty has terrified me" (23:3, 5-6, 15-16). Often we cannot understand why God refrains from intervening. Yet he does not prevent us from crying out, like Jesus on the Cross: "My God, my God, why have you forsaken me?" (*Mt* 27:46). We should continue asking this question in prayerful dialogue before his face: "Lord, holy and true, how long will it be?"

(*Rev* 6:10). It is Saint Augustine who gives us faith's answer to our sufferings: "*Si comprehendis, non est Deus*" — "if you understand him, he is not God." [35] Our protest is not meant to challenge God, or to suggest that error, weakness or indifference can be found in him. For the believer, it is impossible to imagine that God is powerless or that "perhaps he is asleep" (cf. *1 Kg* 18:27). Instead, our crying out is, as it was for Jesus on the Cross, the deepest and most radical way of affirming our faith in his sovereign power. Even in their bewilderment and failure to understand the world around them, Christians continue to believe in the "goodness and loving kindness of God" (*Tit* 3:4). Immersed like everyone else in the dramatic complexity of historical events, they remain unshakably certain that God is our Father and loves us, even when his silence remains incomprehensible.

39. Faith, hope and charity go together. Hope is practised through the virtue of patience, which continues to do good even in the face of

[35] *Sermo* 52, 16: PL 38, 360.

apparent failure, and through the virtue of humility, which accepts God's mystery and trusts him even at times of darkness. Faith tells us that God has given his Son for our sakes and gives us the victorious certainty that it is really true: God is love! It thus transforms our impatience and our doubts into the sure hope that God holds the world in his hands and that, as the dramatic imagery of the end of the Book of Revelation points out, in spite of all darkness he ultimately triumphs in glory. Faith, which sees the love of God revealed in the pierced heart of Jesus on the Cross, gives rise to love. Love is the light — and in the end, the only light — that can always illuminate a world grown dim and give us the courage needed to keep living and working. Love is possible, and we are able to practise it because we are created in the image of God. To experience love and in this way to cause the light of God to enter into the world — this is the invitation I would like to extend with the present Encyclical.

CONCLUSION

40. Finally, let us consider the saints, who exercised charity in an exemplary way. Our thoughts turn especially to Martin of Tours († 397), the soldier who became a monk and a bishop: he is almost like an icon, illustrating the irreplaceable value of the individual testimony to charity. At the gates of Amiens, Martin gave half of his cloak to a poor man: Jesus himself, that night, appeared to him in a dream wearing that cloak, confirming the permanent validity of the Gospel saying: "I was naked and you clothed me ... as you did it to one of the least of these my brethren, you did it to me" (*Mt* 25:36, 40).[36] Yet in the history of the Church, how many other testimonies to charity could be quoted! In partic-

[36] Cf. SULPICIUS SEVERUS, *Vita Sancti Martini*, 3, 1-3: SCh 133, 256-258.

ular, the entire monastic movement, from its origins with Saint Anthony the Abbot († 356), expresses an immense service of charity towards neighbour. In his encounter "face to face" with the God who is Love, the monk senses the impelling need to transform his whole life into service of neighbour, in addition to service of God. This explains the great emphasis on hospitality, refuge and care of the infirm in the vicinity of the monasteries. It also explains the immense initiatives of human welfare and Christian formation, aimed above all at the very poor, who became the object of care firstly for the monastic and mendicant orders, and later for the various male and female religious institutes all through the history of the Church. The figures of saints such as Francis of Assisi, Ignatius of Loyola, John of God, Camillus of Lellis, Vincent de Paul, Louise de Marillac, Giuseppe B. Cottolengo, John Bosco, Luigi Orione, Teresa of Calcutta to name but a few — stand out as lasting models of social charity for all people of good will. The saints are the true bearers of light within history, for they are men and women of faith, hope and love.

41. Outstanding among the saints is Mary, Mother of the Lord and mirror of all holiness. In the *Gospel of Luke* we find her engaged in a service of charity to her cousin Elizabeth, with whom she remained for "about three months" (1:56) so as to assist her in the final phase of her pregnancy. "*Magnificat anima mea Dominum*," she says on the occasion of that visit, "My soul magnifies the Lord" (*Lk* 1:46). In these words she expresses her whole programme of life: not setting herself at the centre, but leaving space for God, who is encountered both in prayer and in service of neighbour — only then does goodness enter the world. Mary's greatness consists in the fact that she wants to magnify God, not herself. She is lowly: her only desire is to be the hand-maid of the Lord (cf. *Lk* 1:38, 48). She knows that she will only contribute to the salvation of the world if, rather than carrying out her own projects, she places herself completely at the disposal of God's initiatives. Mary is a woman of hope: only because she believes in God's promises and awaits the salvation of Israel, can the angel visit her and call her to the decisive service of these promises. Mary is a woman of faith:

"Blessed are you who believed," Elizabeth says to her (cf. *Lk* 1:45). The *Magnificat* — a portrait, so to speak, of her soul — is entirely woven from threads of Holy Scripture, threads drawn from the Word of God. Here we see how completely at home Mary is with the Word of God, with ease she moves in and out of it. She speaks and thinks with the Word of God; the Word of God becomes her word, and her word issues from the Word of God. Here we see how her thoughts are attuned to the thoughts of God, how her will is one with the will of God. Since Mary is completely imbued with the Word of God, she is able to become the Mother of the Word Incarnate. Finally, Mary is a woman who loves. How could it be otherwise? As a believer who in faith thinks with God's thoughts and wills with God's will, she cannot fail to be a woman who loves. We sense this in her quiet gestures, as recounted by the infancy narratives in the Gospel. We see it in the delicacy with which she recognizes the need of the spouses at Cana and makes it known to Jesus. We see it in the humility with which she recedes into the background during Jesus' public life, knowing that the Son must establish a new family and that the Mother's hour will come only with the Cross, which will be Jesus' true hour (cf. *Jn* 2:4; 13:1). When the disciples flee, Mary will remain beneath the Cross (cf. *Jn* 19:25-27); later, at the hour of Pentecost, it will be they who gather around her as they wait for the Holy Spirit (cf. *Acts* 1:14).

42. The lives of the saints are not limited to their earthly biographies but also include their being and working in God after death. In the saints one thing becomes clear: those who draw near to God do not withdraw from men, but rather become truly close to them. In no one do we see this more clearly than in Mary. The words addressed by the crucified Lord to his disciple — to John and through him to all disciples of Jesus: "Behold, your mother!" (*Jn* 19:27) — are fulfilled anew in every generation. Mary has truly become the Mother of all believers. Men and women of every time and place have recourse to her motherly kindness and her virginal purity and grace, in all their needs and aspirations, their joys and sorrows, their moments of loneliness and their common endeavours. They constantly experience the gift of her goodness and the unfailing love which she pours out from the depths of her heart. The testimonials of gratitude, offered to her from every continent and culture, are a recognition of that pure love which is not self-seeking but simply benevolent. At the same time, the devotion of the faithful shows an infallible intuition of how such love is possible: it becomes so as a result of the most intimate union with God, through which the soul is totally pervaded by him — a condition which enables those who have drunk from the fountain of God's love to become in their turn a fountain from which "flow rivers of living water" (*Jn* 7:38). Mary, Virgin and Mother, shows us what love is and whence it draws its origin and its constantly renewed power. To her we entrust the Church and her mission in the service of love:

> Holy Mary, Mother of God,
> you have given the world its true light,
> Jesus, your Son — the Son of God.
> You abandoned yourself completely
> to God's call

and thus became a wellspring
of the goodness
which flows forth from him.
Show us Jesus. Lead us to him.
Teach us to know and love him,
so that we too can become
capable of true love
and be fountains of living water
in the midst of a thirsting world."

Given in Rome, at Saint Peter's, on 25 December, the Solemnity of the Nativity of the Lord, in the year 2005, the first of my Pontificate.

Benedictus PP XVI

INDEX

VATICAN PRESS